THE ROAD TO RESULTS

EFFECTIVE PRACTICES

FOR BUILDING ARTS AUDIENCES

BY **BOB HARLOW**

Cover design by José Moreno

Cover photo by Caiaimage/Martin Barraud

Infographic: Alexander Mostov

Interior design by Tom Starace

Editors: Aaron Dalton and Jennifer Gill

Published by Bob Harlow Research and Consulting, LLC, New York, NY

Library of Congress Control Number: 2014914766

ISBN 978-0-9847287-4-9

Table of Contents

Preface

. . . .

*A*t a time when the arts face new challenges in attracting and re-
taining audiences, arts leaders are eager for information about
what works—and what doesn't—in audience building. Arts
organizations are trying out new ways to increase the size of and diversify
their audiences. Arts service organizations are exploring these topics at
annual conferences. Foundations are funding efforts to find out more.
We believe this study, *The Road to Results: Effective Practices for Building Arts Audiences*, represents an important contribution to this growing
knowledge base.

To get a sense of why, it's useful to look back.

Not quite 15 years ago, The Wallace Foundation asked the RAND
Corporation to review what was known about audience building. The result, published in 2001, was *A New Framework for Building Participation
in the Arts*. Based on an extensive literature review, visits to 13 organizations, and interviews with 102 organizations, the study found that many
efforts by arts organizations to expand audiences suffered from being "hit
or miss." *A New Framework* put forward the idea of a systematic approach, one based on two ideas: that audience-building efforts need to be
aligned with an arts organization's mission, resources, and work; and that
the efforts should focus on removing the particular types of barriers that
stood between the organization and specific target audiences.

Sound ideas, it seemed, but two questions remained:

·· ·· ·· ··

- Could this approach work in practice?
- If yes, how could organizations implement it?

We now have made solid progress toward answering both questions.

Between 2006 and 2012, Wallace funded 54 organizations to develop and test approaches for expanding audiences informed by RAND's guidance. Among the 41 organizations with reliable data, the results were surprisingly positive. For example, over four years, organizations seeking to boost their overall audiences saw median gains of 27 percent. Results for those targeting specific audience segments were even higher, though it's important to note that in some cases organizations were starting from a small base.

This kind of success backed by hard data—unusual in studies of audience-building efforts—was heartening. But for these results to be useful to the field, arts organizations would also need a more detailed understanding of what was behind them. We asked Bob Harlow, a noted market researcher, to take on that task. He looked closely at 10 of the 54 organizations, writing a case study evaluation for each. (Four have been published so far.) *The Road to Results* looks across all 10, and identifies nine practices they shared in common.

As Harlow notes, not all organizations embarked on every single practice, nor did they follow them in a strict sequence. These are key moves—not locksteps.

Think of them as a set of principles to be used with the understanding that each organization's road will look slightly different based on its own unique circumstance.

Like all of Wallace's work, this study reflects our approach to maximizing the impact of our grant making. We work directly with a small number of grantees to help them achieve benefits for their organizations,

· · · · · · · ·

while also capturing and sharing evidence and lessons drawn from their experiences with the goal of benefiting the many similar organizations we are unable to fund.

In addition to the six forthcoming case studies, we'll be publishing a primer by Harlow on using research to support audience-building programs. In the coming years, we'll be tackling new questions, including how audience-building efforts can contribute to arts organizations' financial health.

Why does all of this matter?

Nonprofit arts and cultural organizations play vital roles in providing access to the arts. There is nothing quite like personally observing a dancer's intricate movement on stage, hearing a poignant passage of chamber music or jazz in an acoustically lively hall, feeling an actor's intensity in live dialogue on stage, or seeing a painting with the brushstrokes still visible on the canvas. This remains true even in an age of mobile phones, tablets, home theaters, and 3-D televisions.

We hope *The Road to Results* helps arts organizations across the country tap the experiences of their peers, see how the ideas in the *New Framework* are applied, and begin their own cycles of continuous learning.

Ultimately, we hope that these efforts help introduce more Americans to the pleasure, captivation, and new perspectives that the arts can uniquely provide.

Will Miller

Will Miller
President
The Wallace Foundation

Executive Summary

· · · · · · · ·

*Effective Practices for Successful
Audience Engagement*

Throughout the U.S., arts organizations face a changing and challenging landscape. Americans have more options than ever in ways to spend their leisure time, and younger generations have less exposure to the arts in school than previous generations. They may also want to interact differently with institutions than their parents and grandparents did. The good news is that many arts organizations are learning how to adapt so they can continue to fulfill their missions and even expand their audiences in the process.

This publication details the experiences of 10 such organizations that were among 54 arts institutions that received funding from The Wallace Foundation between 2006 and 2012 to develop audience-building initiatives. An analysis of these programs—each supported by evaluation data—revealed nine practices contributing to their success:

1. Recognizing When Change Is Needed. Organizations saw a pattern of audience behavior that presented an opportunity or a challenge for their financial viability, artistic viability, or both. They recognized that change was necessary to seize this opportunity or overcome the challenge. In some cases, the urgency of the challenge or opportunity actually served the initiative by keeping it front and center, capturing and sustaining the attention of the entire organization over the years needed to build a following.

. . . .

2. *Identifying the Target Audience that Fits.* Compatibility has two meanings here: First, organizations had reason to believe, based either on research or prior experience, that they could make a meaningful connection with the target audience. Second, leaders agreed that serving the audience reinforced—and did not compromise—the organization's other activities or its mission.

3. *Determining What Kinds of Barriers Need to Be Removed.* Successful organizations identified the types of barriers impeding the target audience's participation and shaped their strategies accordingly.

4. *Taking Out the Guesswork: Audience Research to Clarify the Approach.* Organizations often started out knowing very little about the new audience they were targeting and why that audience was not participating. Rather than guess, they went to the source—the target audience itself—for the facts. Using audience research, the organizations gained a clearer understanding of their target group's interests, lifestyles, general attitudes toward the arts, cultural involvement, and opinions of their own institution.

5. *Thinking Through the Relationship.* Some case study organizations went so far as to spell out a vision of the relationship they wanted to cultivate with the new audience, including specific roles for the audience and themselves. By doing so, they gave their audience-building initiatives structure and a sense of purpose. Leaders and staff members understood how they wanted the audience to interact with their organization and developed programs to fulfill that vision.

6. *Providing Multiple Ways In.* Staff expanded the ways people could access their organizations both literally and psychologically. Many orga-

· · · · · · · ·

nizations provided gateway experiences to acquaint newcomers with their activities. Others generated interest by making connections to things that their target audience already knew or by showing them different sides of their institutions.

7. *Aligning the Organization Around the Strategy.* Leaders and staff built clarity, consensus, and internal buy-in around the audience-building initiative's objectives, importance to the organization, and staff roles in implementing it.

8. *Building in Learning.* Even with considerable research and planning, organizations could never be sure that a new audience would react favorably to their overtures. There were stops, starts, and some downright failures along the way. To stay on track and develop a working knowledge of what clicked with their audiences, many of them did on-the-ground experiments or used formal evaluations that drove program improvements.

9. *Preparing for Success.* Success for the 10 organizations involved serving new audiences and assuming new responsibilities. Staff often worked overtime to handle an increased workload. Organizations found that they had to develop new capabilities and refine existing practices to accommodate newcomers, all while continuing to satisfy existing audiences.

Not every institution that was studied implemented each practice, but generally speaking, the more practices they adopted, the greater the success they achieved. Taken together, these practices promoted audience engagement in two ways. First, they created a shared sense of purpose that kept an audience-engagement program front and center for leaders and staff, thus enabling the initiative to permeate a wide range of an organization's activities. Second, the practices helped an arts institution

. . . .

make meaningful connections with its target audience. Staff members developed programs that reflected both the audience's inclinations and the organization's mission and strengths. As a result, they not only engaged the audience, but also fulfilled important objectives for their organization, establishing a cycle that reinforced itself and gave the initiative momentum.

Acknowledgements

I would like to thank several people and organizations for their support over the years of research and analysis underlying this report, starting with my gratitude for the generous support of The Wallace Foundation, and of its staff throughout. Lucas Held, Pam Mendels, and Ann Stone provided guidance for the report and the research behind it. They and their colleagues Rachel Hare Bork, Will Miller, Edward Pauly, Christine Rhee, Jessica Schwartz, and Daniel Windham gave invaluable counsel and encouragement as the report took shape and in reviews of early drafts. I would also like to thank the editors of the report, Aaron Dalton and Jennifer Gill, for bringing out the best in the ideas and examples, and José Moreno of The Wallace Foundation for finding ways to graphically express them. Finally, the staffs of the ten organizations studied—Boston Lyric Opera, The Clay Studio, The Contemporary Jewish Museum, Fleisher Art Memorial, The Isabella Stewart Gardner Museum, Minnesota Opera, Pacific Northwest Ballet, San Francisco Girls Chorus, Seattle Opera, and Steppenwolf Theatre Company—were generous and gracious with both their time and their candor. My heartfelt thanks to all.

Bob Harlow

Introduction

. . . .

*A*udience building is difficult and thoughtful work. Arts organizations looking to build audiences face a changing landscape: Many analyses suggest that fewer Americans have access to arts education today than in prior decades, competition for leisure time is increasing, and new generations of Americans interact differently with institutions than generations past. In light of these trends, many arts organizations are finding ways to adapt so they can continue to fulfill their missions and even expand their audiences. Consider the following:

- The Clay Studio in Philadelphia tripled enrollment and doubled its class revenue in just five years by adding opportunities for hands-on creative experiences that attracted hundreds of young adults to its classes and workshops.

- Fleisher Art Memorial, also in Philadelphia, reacted to rapid demographic changes in its neighborhood by introducing itself in different community settings and creating an inclusive environment at its facility for all who are interested in the arts, including groups that are often underserved by cultural organizations. The number of neighborhood children enrolled in its on-site classes grew 50 percent in four years.

- Seattle's Pacific Northwest Ballet doubled ticket sales to teens in four years, bucking national trends of declining attendance by young people. Its efforts also boosted ticket sales to young adults by 20 percent in the same time period.

Figure 1. Clay Studio Workshop Targeting Young Adults
Photo courtesy of The Clay Studio, Philadelphia

· · · · · · · ·

- Chicago's Steppenwolf Theatre Company responded to a decline in subscriptions by creating a program that strengthened its relationship with single-ticket buyers, and grew repeat visits by 61 percent over three years.

These organizations were among 54 arts groups in six U.S. cities that received funding from The Wallace Foundation's Wallace Excellence Awards (WEA) initiative. The effort, which ran from 2006 to 2012, gave grants to arts organizations to devise and carry out audience-building efforts of their own design. Importantly, the organizations were asked to use research and data both to shape their audience-building programs and to evaluate the results of their work. That evidenced-based approach was expected not only to drive program effectiveness, but also to help identify successful strategies and practices, addressing a need in the field for clearer direction about how to effectively engage audiences.

To that end, 10 organizations representing a variety of art forms were selected for case studies that examined their audience-building programs in detail and evaluated the effectiveness of different practices (see Appendix and Table 2 on pp. 24–25 for further information about them and their programs).[1] Some of the practices deemed effective are most applicable to certain art forms or circumstances. However, an analysis of the case study organizations overall suggests that nine practices (see Figure

---

1. The analysis compared program activities and results against existing theories and principles from the arts and management literature. This "explanatory case study" approach uses structured inquiry and analysis to not only describe organizational programs, but also explain how and why organizations obtained their results. For more on this approach, see Robert K. Yin in *Case Study Research: Design and Methods*, 3rd Edition (New York: Sage Publications, 2003).

· · · · · · · ·

2) promoted audience engagement across a diverse range of initiatives.

The chapters that follow discuss these effective practices, with examples illustrating how they advanced audience-building programs at the case study organizations. It's important to note that not all of the arts groups adopted each practice or carried them out in a similar sequence. Moreover, there may be other practices besides those described here that can help institutions build audiences. Nonetheless, the evidence gathered from the organizations studied strongly suggests that these practices can enhance a wide assortment of audience-building programs.

That's not to say that these initiatives went off without a hitch. Even when the end result was positive, organizations still had to manage their way through considerable trial and error. The bumps in the road, however, were often just as educational as successes, particularly when organizations refined their strategies and tactics in response. That level of detail can be found in the case studies that form the basis of this analysis, available on The Wallace Foundation website (www.wallacefoundation.org).

· · · · · · · · ·

9 Prepare for Success
Plan for the heavier workload and new staff skills that serving new audiences requires.

1 Recognize When Change Is Needed
Respond to audience challenges and opportunities that matter to your organization's future.

8 Build in Learning
Experiment. Evaluate. Adjust. Repeat.

2 Identify the Target Audience that Fits
Focus on a group receptive to your art form and organization, and that leaders agree makes sense to pursue.

7 Align the Organization Around the Strategy
Make sure organization leaders and staff understand and embrace the strategy and their roles in it.

Expanded and Engaged Audiences

3 Determine What Kinds of Barriers Need to be Removed
Are the obstacles between you and the target group practical matters like ticket pricing, people's perceptions or the audience experience itself?

6 Provide Multiple Ways In
Offer a variety of engaging experiences to introduce the target audience to your organization and art form.

4 Take Out the Guesswork
Use audience research to understand the target group's views on your organization and art form.

5 Think Through the Relationship
Develop a vision for how the target audience will interact with your organization.

Figure 2. Nine Effective Practices of Audience-Building Programs

... 1 ...

Recognizing When
Change Is Needed

Successful initiatives were born out of an observation, when staff members saw audience attendance patterns or behaviors that they believed had significant implications for the organization's artistic mission, financial viability, or both. Acknowledging the weight of those implications prompted action and gave the initiatives momentum.

One example comes from The Clay Studio, which provides ceramics instruction and operates a gallery, studio, and retail shop in Philadelphia's Old City arts district. Senior staff members who interact with the public throughout the day recognized that the organization's audience was not growing. The institution was not only serving the same demographic—well-educated middle-aged or older patrons—but also welcoming the *same people* day after day, month after month. Seeing so few new faces even at special exhibitions "panicked us a little," says Jeff Guido, artistic director at the time. Staff knew that The Clay Studio's future depended on growing its base of visitors, but where would they find them and how would they attract them? This concern kick-started an initiative that ultimately succeeded in drawing hundreds of young adults to workshops and classes.

Chicago's Steppenwolf Theatre Company spotted a disturbing trend

· · · · · · · ·

by analyzing ticket receipts: Despite having a subscription base and renewal rate higher than those of most regional theaters, it saw its total
number of subscribers decline due to a significant drop in acquiring new
ones. Knowing that performing arts organizations across the country
were seeing similar declines, Steppenwolf staff did not think they could
turn the tide and acquire large numbers of new subscribers. They also recognized, however, that they could not simply acquiesce to further audience attrition. Instead, Steppenwolf believed it was necessary to cultivate
a different kind of loyalty outside of the traditional subscription model.
This realization mobilized staff to implement a very successful program
that engaged single-ticket buyers (and subscribers) and brought them to
the theater more often.

Making art accessible to all has been the mission of the Fleisher Art
Memorial in Philadelphia since its establishment in the late 19th century.
Founder Samuel Fleisher pictured a place where people from different
cultures, backgrounds, and artistic experiences in the surrounding community could create art side by side.

Heading into the 21st century, Fleisher ran classes and workshops in
its large South Philadelphia facility, as well as off-site programs in schools
and community centers. Different staff members managed on-site and
off-site programs until a reorganization made some individuals responsible for both. These staff members now had the perspective to see that
students in Fleisher's off-site programs tended to be very ethnically diverse—a reflection of the diversity in the surrounding neighborhoods—
and include many newly arrived immigrants. Meanwhile students in its
on-site programs were primarily white and from more affluent Philadelphia neighborhoods and suburbs. This divide concerned the staff because

· · · · · · · ·

it went against Samuel Fleisher's vision of bringing together people of diverse backgrounds and providing access to the arts. The organization channeled that concern into a successful initiative that is beginning to attract more students and visitors from its ethnically diverse neighborhood to on-site programs. As with most diversity efforts, progress has been slow but steady. Keeping the faith could easily be a challenge, but the importance of this initiative to Fleisher's mission strengthens staff members' resolve and helps them to persevere.

The Clay Studio, Steppenwolf, and Fleisher made their observations in different ways: through on-the-ground experience, analysis of ticket receipts, and gaining the fresh perspective of an internal reorganization. What they have in common is that their observations captured the attention of their entire organizations because they revealed genuine threats to missions or financial sustainability that could not be ignored.

In fact, some top management experts believe that organizational change can only get traction when it invokes a sense of urgency based on a realistic appraisal of opportunities and hazards.[2] That urgency galvanizes leadership to initiate and commit to a course of action. In addition, serving "new audiences" (a term used throughout this report

> *The observations captured the organizations' attention because they revealed threats to missions or financial sustainability, creating a sense of urgency.*

---

2. See, for example, John P. Kotter, *Leading Change* (Boston: Harvard Business School Press, 1996), for a discussion of the role of urgency, including the distinction between real urgency and a false urgency that gives the appearance of movement, but does not produce lasting change. See also John P. Kotter, "Leading Change: Why Transformation Efforts Fail," *Harvard Business Review* 73 (1995), 59–67.

· · · · · · · ·

to mean audiences who are new to a particular organization) inevitably requires focusing on different objectives and doing some things different-ly. A sense of urgency combats complacency and motivates staff to move beyond their comfort zones.

This does not mean arts groups should succumb to hysteria over imagined or manufactured crises. The observations at The Clay Studio, Steppenwolf, and Fleisher were grounded in organizational and environ-mental realities, often complemented by knowledge of broader audience trends. The sense of urgency came naturally because staff members un-derstood that they faced a bona fide challenge or opportunity with major consequences for their organization's future.

Leaders with insight and vision often played instrumental roles in channeling that urgency into productive action at the case study organi-zations. Consider, for instance, Pacific Northwest Ballet's (PNB) artistic director, Peter Boal, who recognized that the company had to confront national trends of declining ballet attendance among young people. He confessed that his "darkest fear" was ballet disappearing in a century's time if it did not attract the next generation of supporters. Boal chan-neled that fear into an alternate vision for ballet that the rest of the staff could get behind. "There are certain performing arts that young audienc-es *do* care about," says Boal. "They care about hearing a musical group. They care about certain films. I want ballet to be in that category." Fueled by zeal and a sense of possibility, PNB has succeeded in attracting large numbers of young audience members to its performances, bucking na-tional trends.

Figure 3. Artistic Director Peter Boal Leads Pacific Northwest Ballet's Teen Night
Photo by Rex Tranter; Courtesy of Pacific Northwest Ballet, Seattle

2

Identifying the Target
Audience that Fits

*I*t is no surprise that successful audience-building initiatives target a *specific audience*. After all, it is hard to address attendance barriers or build a meaningful connection with people using a one-size-fits-all strategy.

At some case study organizations, the mission-critical observation prompting the initiative implied a specific audience. When Fleisher Art Memorial discovered that newly arrived immigrants living in the surrounding area were not coming to its on-site programs, it presented a clear challenge to target them in order to fulfill its mission as a community arts organization. Pacific Northwest Ballet, meanwhile, naturally focused its attention on young audiences because of the concerns of Boal and other staff members about the nationwide decline in ballet attendance among young people.

The target audience wasn't so obvious for many of the other arts groups. Figuring it out required both creativity and strategic thinking. In the end, they asked themselves two critical questions:

· · · · · · · ·

1. Is the audience likely to be receptive?
2. Do leaders agree the audience is important to the organization?

Receptive Audiences

Case study organizations pursued audiences that research or past experience led them to believe they could satisfy.

Steppenwolf could have tried recruiting new subscribers to prop up the decline in its base, but it realized it would be tough going in light of a national trend away from theater subscriptions. It also could have pursued new single-ticket buyers. But staff members knew that the high costs of acquiring new single-ticket buyers and the challenges of converting them into returning patrons could very well yield a poor return on investment.

That's when Steppenwolf turned to research to identify how to foster greater loyalty from its current audience. The focus group research revealed that Steppenwolf's single-ticket buyers identified just as strongly with the theater as subscribers did. They considered Steppenwolf *their* theater. They believed the company produced challenging, thought-provoking work, and they saw themselves as lifelong learners who attended its productions to expand their intellectual boundaries.

Single-ticket buyers were certainly a willing audience—after all, they were already coming—but how could Steppenwolf encourage them to come more often? Steppenwolf opted to capitalize on the desire for intellectual stimulation that brought these people to the theater in the first place. Senior leaders noted a parallel between the intellectual experience that single-ticket buyers were seeking and the types of conversations that

. . . .

took place among the company's ensemble as they readied productions for the stage. They saw an opportunity to strengthen the theater's connection with single-ticket buyers (and all other audience members) by bringing them into those conversations via a variety of online and in-person forums. Steppenwolf's audience-engagement program yielded impressive results. In three years, the number of non-subscribers who purchased tickets to more than one performance grew by 61 percent (and subscriber renewal rates also rose slightly).

Past experience with an audience can also reveal new possibilities. When The Contemporary Jewish Museum (CJM) moved from a 2,500-square-foot space to a 63,000-square-foot facility, Connie Wolf, president and CEO at the time, naturally felt pressure to fill it with visitors. She recalled her experience as director of education at New York's Whitney Museum and how families made the museum feel dynamic. "The stuffiness of a museum immediately exits the minute families walk in the door," she says. Moreover, she saw how many families made the Whitney their personal space, returning time and again as loyal visitors.

Wolf envisioned a central role for families in The CJM's new home, and her staff built programs to achieve that vision. They organized exhibits that would appeal to both adults and children, and developed family-oriented tours, artist-led art-making activities for kids, and other activities that families could enjoy together. They created a family-friendly environment with seating nooks and other areas where parents and children could read, draw, or just take a moment to refresh themselves. They also forged a series of partnerships with preschools and elementary schools that involved not only teachers and students, but also parents in workshops and museum visits. Within four years, The CJM was

· · · · · · · ·

welcoming more than 22,000 families a year, compared to 1,300 in its previous facility. Families went from 10 percent of all visitors to 18 percent.

Sometimes, it's possible to stumble on a responsive audience by chance and seize an opportunity. Lani Willis, senior marketing and communications director of the Minnesota Opera, wasn't thinking about a long-term audience-building strategy when she had less than 48 hours to fill the house for a Tuesday night performance of an obscure work by an obscure composer (Reinhard Keiser's *The Fortunes of King Croesus*). Taking advantage of a previously scheduled PR engagement, she partnered with Ian Punnett, a popular local radio talk show host. Punnett spoke about his own love for opera as he gave away 500 free performance tickets to his listeners, many of whom had never attended an opera before. Willis not only filled the house, but also made a serendipitous discovery: The opera novices thoroughly enjoyed themselves, despite the fact that they were not attending *Carmen*, *La Bohème*, or the handful of operas seen as suitable for beginners. Armed with that knowledge, Willis hatched the idea of leveraging Punnett's rapport with the mostly female listeners of his pop-culture radio show to build the organization's audience of women ages 35 to 60. Using a combination of ticket giveaways and Punnett's ongoing banter about the opera and why he enjoyed it, the company was able to chip away at preconceptions that non-operagoers had about the art form. Hundreds of Punnett's listeners, many of them in the target audience, responded to the call during the four-year initiative, and many continue to attend Minnesota Opera performances.

These three organizations pursued audiences that research (Steppenwolf) or experience (The CJM and Minnesota Opera) gave them reason to believe they could satisfy. Other organizations drew on their

. . . .

knowledge of broader trends, as the Isabella Stewart Gardner Museum did when it considered young adults' penchant for social activities in designing *Gardner After Hours*, an event that draws hundreds of young adults to the museum each month. That said, some arts groups did build momentum with particular audiences even when knowledge or experience suggested an uphill battle. Pacific Northwest Ballet (PNB) suspected that attracting teens and young adults would require dispelling their image of ballet as boring and stuffy, and did not see immediately how it would accomplish that. The organization ultimately used audience research (covered in "Taking Out the Guesswork: Audience Research to Clarify the Approach," pp. 30–32) to discover the best pathways.

Leaders Must Agree the Target Audience Is a Priority

Importantly, leaders need to agree that a particular audience, and the programs and activities developed to serve it, align with the organization's mission and identity. Without that support, momentum will stall.[3] At one performing arts organization, for example, an initiative led by the marketing department attracted many new patrons, but efforts to re-engage them were stifled when others in the institution resisted efforts to change the wording in some advertising to make the art form more

---

3. Management scholar Zannie Voss and her colleagues have demonstrated what many arts managers suspect—when leaders responsible for managing different parts of a theater do not share the same view of its values and commitments, success (as measured by ticket revenue and net income) suffers. See Zannie Voss, Daniel M. Cable, and Glenn B. Voss, "Organizational Identity and Firm Performance: What Happens When Leaders Disagree About 'Who We Are'?" *Organization Science* 17 (2006), 741–755.

. . . .

accessible to newcomers. Those who objected did so because they believed the new copy "dumbed down" how they spoke to the public. At
the core of the dispute was a lack of consensus on the importance of this
audience to the organization's future.

At that organization and some others, executive directors did not
seem to have a clear sense of why a target audience mattered, nor did
the initiative capture the attention of many department heads. When
leaders did agree about an audience's importance, they rallied their organizations to make audiences feel welcome and provide different ways
for them to connect with the art. That kind of consensus may be easiest
to achieve when initiatives mesh with the organization's core values (e.g.,
Steppenwolf) or are linked to a mission that ignites passion in leaders
(e.g., Fleisher).

····3····

Determining What Kinds of
Barriers Need to Be Removed

*T*o succeed, case study organizations recognized that they had to address the relevant barriers standing between them and their target audiences. That is no small task, especially when an arts group is pursuing an audience that it knows little about. There may be many reasons why a particular audience isn't coming. How can an organization begin to identify the most important ones?

In the RAND Corporation's *A New Framework for Building Participation in the Arts*, researchers Kevin P. McCarthy and Kimberly Jinnett offer a way to bring clarity to the challenge. They reviewed scores of audience-building programs and a broad literature base to develop a model that explains why people become involved in the arts. The model specifies the different factors that determine an audience's decision to participate in the arts, and how to influence them. It categorizes people into one of three groups depending on their current commitment to the arts, and posits that successful engagement efforts require strategies and tactics that address specific factors relevant to each group (see Table 1).[4]

---

4. The original *New Framework* model discusses a person's proclivity to engage in the arts as a whole, as opposed to one particular art form. We believe that the model has greatest utility if it is used instead to consider a person's proclivity to engage in specific art forms, simply because people are not predisposed to engage equally in all of

· · · · · · · ·

1. People who are *disinclined* have little interest in the arts. They
    likely keep their distance from arts organizations because of
    perceptual barriers. For example, they might believe an art form
    has nothing to offer or think that they'd feel out of place in a
    venue such as an opera house, gallery, or museum. Since their
    mindset differs from that of current patrons, attracting them
    would *diversify* and change the composition of an organization's
    audience. In this context, diversification does not mean a demo-
    graphic change, such as in age, ethnicity, or gender, but a shift in
    the psychographic profile of an organization's audience.

2. The *inclined*, meanwhile, see value in participating in an art form
    but aren't currently doing so. RAND's *New Framework* posits
    that *practical barriers*, such as a lack of money, time, or transpor-
    tation, are likely keeping them away. People who are inclined to
    participate probably have a lot in common with current visitors.
    At a minimum, they share the belief that the art form is reward-
    ing. Targeting them would *broaden* an organization's audience
    because they are similar to existing audience members.

3. Finally, there is an organization's *current audience*. According to
    the *New Framework*, arts groups can *deepen* the involvement of
    current patrons by making their *experience* more satisfying in
    some way. (See sidebar on p. 22 for examples of all three types of
    audience-building challenges from organizations profiled in the
    case studies.)

---

them. The full report, *A New Framework for Building Participation in the Arts* (Santa
Monica, CA: RAND Corp., 2001), is available at http://www.wallacefoundation.org/
knowledge-center/audience-development-for-the-arts/key-research/Documents/New-
Framework-for-Building-Participation-in-the-Arts.pdf.

· · · · · · · ·

Target Audience	Audience-Building Goal	Relevant Factors
Disinclined	Diversify	Perceptual
Inclined	Broaden	Practical
Current Audience	Deepen	Experience

Table 1. Alignment Among Target Audience, Goals, and Relevant Factors as per RAND's New Framework

Results from the programs that were studied are consistent with the *New Framework*. The arts organizations found that addressing perceptions was the key to attracting disinclined audiences, removing practical barriers boosted participation among inclined audiences, and improving the experience could increase visits from current audiences.

To illustrate this point, Figure 4 lists the 10 case study organizations and their audience-building goals, strategies, and results in the context of the *New Framework*. The first three columns use the *New Framework* to categorize each organization's audience-building goal—Broadening, Deepening, Diversifying, or some combination.[5] The middle columns indicate the participation barriers that the organizations targeted. The last three columns show where the initiatives succeeded. Organizations typically fulfilled their objectives when they targeted the relevant barriers suggested by the *New Framework*.

Table 2 provides greater detail about each organization's objective, strategy, programs, tactics, and results. With the exception of Steppenwolf Theatre Company, all of the case study organizations sought to

---

5. Classified by the author using the *New Framework* definitions.

· · · · · · · ·

Diversifying, Broadening, and Deepening: Examples from the Field

Diversifying: The San Francisco Girls Chorus (SFGC) wanted to expand its concert audience, which largely consisted of chorus members' friends and family. Its target was "classical music patrons," a group defined by its regular attendance at classical music performances such as symphony or chamber music concerts. Classical music patrons had a demographic profile similar to SFGC's current audience members, but they weren't inclined to attend its concerts in large numbers. To attract them—and therefore diversify its audience—SFGC sought to change their perception of both girls' choral music and the artistic level of the organization itself.

Broadening: The Boston Lyric Opera (BLO) believed that there was a potential audience of young parents in the suburbs who were interested in attending the opera, but were kept away by a lack of time to go into the city to see a performance and the need to arrange for child care. BLO successfully lowered those practical barriers and welcomed thousands of inclined audience members and their children by presenting "family performances" in suburbs with a high concentration of opera fans. These family performances were abridged versions of full-length operas featuring professional singers and orchestra.

Deepening: Steppenwolf Theatre Company sought to increase repeat attendance among current single-ticket buyers. To do so, it enhanced the experience of going to the theater by creating online and in-person forums where audience members could explore the meaning of the work on stage.

	Audience-Building Goal			Target Factors			Success		
	Broaden	Deepen	Diversify	Practical	Experience	Perceptual	Broaden	Deepen	Diversify
Boston Lyric Opera									
The Clay Studio									
The Contemporary Jewish Museum									
Fleisher Art Memorial									
Isabella Stewart Gardner Museum									
Minnesota Opera									
Pacific Northwest Ballet									
San Francisco Girls Chorus									
Seattle Opera									
Steppenwolf Theatre Company									

Figure 4. Audience-Building Goals, Strategies, and Results

attract new audiences. They often acted on hunches about whether the audience they were targeting was inclined or disinclined, and those hunches were mostly accurate. Many WEA grantees also did audience research to confirm their educated guesses and get more precise reads on the most influential barriers and how to address them (discussed in the next section).

The Boston Lyric Opera (BLO) is an interesting case in the context of the *New Framework* because it pursued two different audiences with the same tactics. BLO originally planned to take abridged family-friendly versions of its opera productions into suburbs where a large number of opera-*inclined* parents lived. In doing so, it hoped to address *practical* barriers (i.e., distance, cost, and time) that had kept them from

· · · · · · · ·

Table 2. Organizations' Initiatives in the Context of RAND's *New Framework*

Organization	Objective	Strategy	Programs/Tactics	Result
Boston Lyric Opera	*Broaden (and, midway through the initiative, Diversify).* Attract families to opera.	Create opportunities for parents to share opera with their children.	Present abridged "family-friendly" versions of popular operas in Boston and its suburbs.	High attendance in neighborhoods with a strong opera following, less so in areas without a preexisting fan base.
The Clay Studio	*Diversify.* Attract and retain urban professionals ages 25 to 45, including singles and parents.	Develop new class and event formats that align with how young adults spend their free time.	Offer social workshops as low-pressure introductions to working with clay. Create shorter, less expensive courses that accommodate a range of budgets and schedules.	Doubled the revenue of the school in five years.
The Contemporary Jewish Museum	*Broaden and Diversify.* Attract families to the museum for long and satisfying visits with at least 40% coming from ethnically diverse, low-income, or LGBTQ groups in San Francisco.	Eliminate financial barriers, raise awareness, create programs for families, and include family-focused exhibitions in the annual schedule.	Present annual family-focused shows, targeted family marketing, free admission for children 18 and under every day and free admission for families on select days each year, offer scheduled and drop-in family programs, build partnerships with schools and public libraries.	Attracted tens of thousands of families each year, with nearly one-third coming from underrepresented demographic groups.
Fleisher Art Memorial	*Diversify.* Attract residents of the surrounding ethnically diverse neighborhood to on-site programs.	Raise awareness, increase familiarity, and build goodwill in the neighborhood.	Build on preexisting relationships with community groups, hire community liaisons, and raise the organization's profile through artist residencies in local parks, art making at community festivals, and other activities.	Neighborhood youth in on-site youth/child programs went from 25% of the students to 36%.
Isabella Stewart Gardner Museum	*Broaden and Diversify.* Attract young Boston professionals, many of whom may not currently visit due to schedule conflicts with the museum's limited opening hours.	Tap into young adults' desire to be social and at the same time draw them into the art collection.	Host a monthly evening event with a variety of brief educational programs in a social and informal atmosphere designed to encourage appreciation of the collection.	Attracted capacity crowds of young adults (up to 800 each month) who socialized and explored the galleries.

· · · · · · · ·

Organization	Objective	Strategy	Programs/Tactics	Result
Minnesota Opera	*Diversify.* Attract and retain women ages 35 to 60 who are newcomers to opera.	Dispel perceptions of opera as stuffy and elitist.	Form a long-term partnership with the host of a local women's talk radio show. Have him share his enthusiasm for opera through an integrated and strategic campaign of on-air promotions, ticket giveaways, opera house events and interviews.	Large numbers of newcomers from the target demographic attended the opera on a comp ticket, with 18% purchasing a ticket for a subsequent performance.
Pacific Northwest Ballet	*Diversify.* Attract teens and young adults to the ballet.	(1) Offer reduced-price tickets, (2) help young adults get to know PNB, and (3) change their perception of the company from stodgy and distant to exciting and approachable.	Expand digital presence with extensive multimedia content and update marketing materials.	Ticket sales to teens doubled and sales to 18- to 25-year-olds rose 20%.
San Francisco Girls Chorus	*Diversify.* Attract classical music aficionados to its concerts, which were attended mainly by the friends and family of chorus members.	Change perceptions about girls' choral music.	Revise marketing and concert presentation to better project an image of artistic excellence and to align with the expectations and experiences of classical music patrons.	Classical music patrons who were not affiliated with a chorus member rose from 18% of the audience to 28%.
Seattle Opera	*Broaden, Deepen, and Diversify.* Deepen the experience of attending the opera for existing audiences, use a free simulcast to attract newcomers to a performance, and reconnect with lapsed patrons.	Use technology to deliver a deeper intellectual experience for existing audiences and to take opera beyond its usual opera hall context for new audiences.	Use behind-the-scenes videos, interactive forums, apps, and other digital tools to expose audiences to different aspects of the work on stage and present a free simulcast in a local arena to entice new audiences and reconnect with patrons who may not have attended recently.	Created a richer experience for thousands of current operagoers and attracted thousands of newcomers to the opera.
Steppenwolf Theatre Company	*Deepen.* Encourage existing single-ticket buyers to attend more performances.	Create a more intellectually stimulating experience.	Extend the ensemble artists' dialogue about the work beyond the stage to reach audience members in online and in-person venues.	Repeat visits from single-ticket buyers increased 61%.

· · · · · · · ·

attending the opera. The strategy worked, and thousands of families in those communities enjoyed its performances. Due to unforeseen logistical circumstances and venue availability issues, BLO also performed in some suburbs that did not have a strong opera following. To attract audiences in these communities, it needed to overcome *perceptual* barriers among *disinclined* individuals. Unfortunately, BLO had neither the time nor resources to do so. It addressed the same practical barriers that worked with inclined audiences, but the strategy was a mismatch and it played to houses that were more than half empty in those markets.

BLO's experience reveals the power of the *New Framework* as a guide to determining which barriers to address. That said, McCarthy and Jinnett acknowledge that in reducing a complex process to three broad categories of audiences, the model runs the risk of oversimplifying which barriers are relevant for which ones. Many audiences, especially disinclined ones, may face more than one kind of barrier. Even if a disinclined individual changes his mind and is willing to give an organization and its art a try, practical barriers such as a lack of time may still be impediments.[6]

Moreover, the *New Framework* does not encompass interactions between barriers. For example, a high admission price (which the model would consider a practical barrier) can signal to disinclined audiences that the art is not for them, thus inadvertently reinforcing their percep-

---

6. The model itself acknowledges this specific possibility; it is sequential in that individuals move from being disinclined to inclined to participate. That means a disinclined audience may have practical barriers in addition to perceptual ones.

. . . .

tual barriers.[7] Conversely, Seattle Opera, Minnesota Opera, and The Clay Studio all found that eliminating or reducing prices can weaken the power of perceptual barriers. Thousands of people who were new to opera or very infrequent attendees came to Seattle Opera's free simulcast of a performance. Hundreds of women who had never been to the opera set aside preconceptions that it was stuffy and elitist when the Minnesota Opera offered them a free ticket. Hundreds of newcomers signed up when The Clay Studio added shorter, inexpensive classes. For these target audiences, a lower cost—or no cost at all—mitigated the risk of taking a chance on something new that they were not sure they would enjoy. Once the price dropped, they figured they had nothing to lose.

These exceptions do not detract from the *New Framework*'s value as a guide to understanding the barriers likely to be most salient to a particular audience. The experiences of the case study organizations largely aligned with the model. It is important, however, not to interpret the *New Framework*'s guidance as a prescription.

---

7. See, e.g., Jennifer Wiggins, "Motivation, Ability, and Opportunity to Participate: A Reconceptualization of the RAND Model of Audience Development," *International Journal of Arts Management* 7 (Fall 2004), 22–33.

···*4*···

Taking Out the Guesswork: Audience Research to Clarify the Approach

*M*ost of the organizations studied pursued new audiences they knew little about. They didn't know what the audience thought of their art form or organization, or how cultural activities fit into their lives. Audience research was essential to pinning down specific barriers to participation, identifying tactics to address them, and finding aspects of their organization that excited newcomers. Each area is covered below.

Pinning Down the Barriers

The case study organizations found research most helpful when it explored the factors that RAND's *New Framework* specified as most relevant for their particular audience: perceptual factors for disinclined audiences, practical factors for inclined audiences, and experiential factors for current audiences. Steppenwolf Theatre Company, for instance, knew it wanted to create programs for single-ticket buyers (a segment of its current audience) that enhanced their experience of attending the

· · · · · · · ·

theater. Accordingly, the organization didn't waste time with focus groups discussing practical barriers such as price, parking, or promotions. Instead, it concentrated on the audience experience to understand why single-ticket buyers attended performances and the role the organization played in their intellectual lives.

Because most of the institutions pursued disinclined audiences, research that focused on understanding how the target group perceived them and their art forms proved most valuable in sharpening strategy and building out tactics. This inquiry is critical—too many arts organizations skip this step and limit their success with disinclined audiences. A few basic questions proved particularly useful in clarifying perceptual barriers:

- What does this audience know about our art form and about us—or what do they think they know?
- How do those perceptions align with the audience's cultural and leisure time priorities?
- Do our website, brochures, and other marketing materials attract their attention? What messages do they send?

Time and again, research reveals that the biggest barriers for a disinclined audience are indifference and low familiarity, often coupled with a perception of the organization as elitist. That's exactly what Pacific Northwest Ballet (PNB) found. It conducted several focus groups with young people to understand what they thought of ballet and PNB and how those perceptions influenced their decision to attend or not. The research revealed that young people weren't coming because they thought ballet was elitist, boring, and stuffy. They assumed that they wouldn't appreciate a performance because they lacked in-depth knowledge about ballet. They also didn't know what to expect if they did attend a performance.

. . . .

To some extent, PNB's marketing and website unintentionally reinforced those perceptions. Focus group participants reviewed the organization's marketing and found it less than appealing. For starters, the advertising lacked information about ticket prices, leading them to assume that tickets would be expensive and scarce. The ads also featured sterile, faraway shots of dancers, which demonstrated their technical prowess but failed to connect on an emotional level with young people. Nothing pulled them in.

PNB staff found it difficult to hear such feedback, but they came away with a clear sense of direction: They needed to infuse their marketing with the excitement of the live experience and communicate the inclusiveness of the organization. They also had to dispel some of the mystery surrounding PNB by helping young audiences get to know the

Facing Uncomfortable Truths

It is not easy to sit behind a one-way mirror at a focus group facility and listen to people criticizing your organization or art form when they've never tried either one. Some staff members may even want to forgo research to avoid hearing it. While it may be easy to say, "They just don't get it!" and walk away, Pacific Northwest Ballet and other case study organizations discovered that negative opinions cannot be discounted or ignored. They represent strong barriers that must be overcome in order to convert a disinclined audience. Keep in mind, too, that a potential new audience's perceptions usually are not based on experience. After all, they are not currently attending! They may not react favorably to your marketing materials and that's okay—they weren't designed for them.

company. Guided by the research findings, PNB revamped its print advertising to include close-ups of dancers with clear facial expressions that depicted emotions associated with their characters, to convey a sense of immediacy. Staff also made it a strategic priority to produce online videos that showed different sides of the company, its repertoire, and its artists. These videos introduced audiences of all ages to PNB and provided an idea of what it would be like to see a performance.

It can be tempting to avoid research altogether and move right away to the "real work" of developing and implementing programs. For starters, research can be expensive. It also can easily add several months to project timelines. If that's not enough, it can simply be difficult to hear what target audiences think of an organization and if that organization is even on their radar (see sidebar, "Facing Uncomfortable Truths").

However, if an arts group has not had much prior success with an audience it wants to target, questions of organizational and artistic relevance with that audience need to be addressed first. Fleisher Art Memorial learned this when it set out to attract recent immigrants and other neighborhood residents underserved by the organization. At the start of their initiative, Fleisher staff didn't recognize the extent of the organization's relevance problem. They put ideas together for programs that they hoped would bring in more local residents, including a summer camp and free family workshops. Later, staff sought input from community leaders and current students from the neighborhood about how to structure those programs, and got some unexpected feedback: No matter how much Fleisher was admired by its existing students and leaders of community organizations, most members of the neighborhood's underserved groups, regardless of their interest in the arts, didn't know or care

· · · · · · · ·

what Fleisher was. The organization could build the programs, but it was unlikely that large numbers of its target audience would come no matter how they were designed.

Staff shelved the programming ideas and instead did focus groups with neighborhood residents from underserved groups to better understand how to build trust and relevance with them. They found that, instead of feeling welcome, many saw Fleisher as an institution that catered to people who were only interested in Western European art and had time and money to spare. While residents were interested in enrichment programs for their children, they were unlikely to bring them to Fleisher because they didn't think they would fit in.

These insights led Fleisher to take several steps to introduce itself to the community in vivid ways, including a mobile studio that brings art making to neighborhood parks, festivals, and schools, and a Teen Lounge at its facility so youth can drop in to make art as their schedules and transportation logistics permit. Fleisher even takes over its block and an adjacent small park for its annual street festival, *ARTspiration!*, giving hundreds of neighbors a chance to spend the day engaged in art-making activities.

Designing Tactics to Address the Barriers

Even small research projects can uncover barriers and provide detailed guidance on overcoming them. The San Francisco Girls Chorus (SFGC) has won classical music Grammy and ASCAP awards for its artistic excellence and even sang at the 2009 inauguration of President Obama. So imagine the dismay of staffers when three focus groups of classical music

· · · · · · · ·

patrons told them that the phrase "girls chorus" conjured up images of a glee club singing Disney tunes in a church basement. Chorus staff had suspected that such perceptions were widely held—indeed, some staff members had been wary of audience research because they didn't want their suspicions confirmed. But they also believed that it was important to the Chorus's future to expand its audience beyond friends and family members of choristers and attract local classical music lovers. With that in mind, they plunged into research to pinpoint the origins of these perceptions and how to change them.

It turned out that SFGC's own marketing materials had buttressed some stereotypical misperceptions. For example, focus groups of patrons of other San Francisco classical music organizations thought a group photo of the girls on the home page of SFGC's website made them look more like a class on a school trip than an award-winning ensemble (Figure 5, top). They did, however, react positively to informal close-up shots of SFGC members in performance that highlighted their emotions, or small group photos (Figure 5, bottom). Applying this information, SFGC replaced group photos of the girls in its brochures, postcards, and website with more intimate group shots and images of individual girls in performance.

The focus groups also revealed potential issues with the way SFGC presented its performances. The Chorus did actually hold some of its concerts in churches—and not in the subset of Bay Area churches that classical music patrons recognized as professional venues. Moreover, the organization relied on volunteer ushers who did not wear uniforms and were sometimes difficult to differentiate from audience members. Classical music patrons were accustomed to attending performances in established venues with professional-looking front-of-house staffs.

· · · · · · · ·

Figure 5. SFGC Images Presented to Focus Group Respondents
Photos courtesy of San Francisco Girls Chorus

· · · · · · · ·

Based on this insight, SFGC moved its performances to more established venues with a professional box office and signage. It implemented a dress code for front-of-house staff so they could be easily distinguished from audience members. The organization also made performance enhancements, such as inviting guest artists to concerts and upgrading its lighting and audiovisual capabilities. After making these changes, SFGC succeeded in attracting more classical music patrons than ever before. Its well-designed market research (see sidebar, "Research with a Purpose") was the catalyst that enabled it.

The experiences of Pacific Northwest Ballet and SFGC highlight an important point: Marketing messages—and even photographs—that appeal to existing audiences may have limited pull and even alienate potential newcomers who are less familiar with an organization, its art, and the lingo used by experienced insiders. In a worst-case scenario, marketing materials can accidentally strengthen perceptual barriers or make new people feel that they lack the necessary knowledge or experience to appreciate a visit. Research can identify these issues.

Identifying What Excites Newcomers

Audience research also helped organizations identify aspects of themselves and their art that piqued the interest of newcomers. Sometimes, staff discovered that they and the new audience weren't passionate about the same things. Staff at The Clay Studio were enamored with the beautiful objects on display in their shop and galleries, and featured them prominently in marketing materials. The organization is also proud of its international reputation for advancing the ceramic arts. These things

· · · · · · · ·

Research with a Purpose

All too often, research gets done and then collects dust on a shelf because people are not sure how to act on it. There are a couple of possible reasons why. Sometimes, the research covers issues of questionable importance to the organization or things that it can't affect. In other cases, the research identifies critical issues but does not give guidance on how to address them. The organizations profiled in case studies got the greatest value from research when they focused their inquiries on things they could change or improve. Once the results were in, they thought through the implications of the findings and potential courses of action.

The San Francisco Girls Chorus (SFGC) got so much mileage out of its audience research because Executive Director Melanie Smith focused it tightly on what was keeping classical music patrons away from its performances. But that wasn't all. Smith and her staff also used research to figure out how to change those perceptions that were problematic. So, for instance, they explored in detail how well elements of their marketing, front-of-house experience, and onstage presentation aligned with what classical music patrons expected from organizations known for artistic excellence. They also asked focus groups to critique their website and brochures.

With a limited budget (a constraint faced by most arts organizations) and just a few focus groups, SFGC recognized that it could not afford to waste time or money on general questions about performing arts attendance or even preferred music genres. That kind of research likely would have garnered little attention in the organization because those were not elements likely to be acted on—interesting to know, but soon forgotten.

· · · · · · · ·

held little sway with focus groups of young adults who were not familiar with the organization. What did excite them was the idea of working hands-on with clay. Former President and CEO Amy Sarner Williams recalls the reactions of young adults to marketing materials in focus groups:

> We had this tagline, "Shaping the future of ceramics," which was great but that was for us. Not so much for the audience. That was a real eye-opener. People would say to us in focus groups, "Why would I look at this? Why would that make me want to come? I've got to look at something and right away see there's something there for me."

Taking that cue, The Clay Studio modified its advertising for this audience to focus less on its place in the art world and beautiful ceramic objects, and more on the experiences people could have at the organization. Staff added more action words to the copy and photographs of people working with clay. They also sought other ways to showcase the experience of working with clay, including demonstrations by resident artists and featuring an artist's working studio as part of an exhibition to show visitors a rarely seen side of the process. The strategy has reeled in many new visitors to The Clay Studio, which at the same time remains committed to activities that support its stature in the ceramic art community.

Detailed descriptions of specific audience-research projects and supporting research materials can be found in the upcoming companion volume, *Taking Out the Guesswork: Using Research to Build Arts Audiences*, available in 2015 at www.wallacefoundation.org.

. . . .

Low-Cost Alternatives to Formal Research

The reality is that many arts organizations work with tight budgets and may not be able to afford the services of a professional market research firm. Even a small research project, such as a few focus groups, might be out of reach. Some case study organizations took novel, low-cost approaches to learn about new audiences and gained invaluable strategic guidance for their initiatives.

Staff at the Isabella Stewart Gardner Museum, for instance, didn't have the budget for professionally moderated focus groups but still wanted feedback to develop and refine programming and marketing ideas for *Gardner After Hours*, a new monthly evening event targeting young urban professionals. Instead, they recruited three groups of museum volunteers and staff ages 18 to 34 to take part in discussions after work with pizza and refreshments. Led by a staff member, the participants discussed the kinds of after-work events they and their friends enjoyed. They also reacted to programming ideas for the event and brainstormed other ways to involve young visitors with the museum's collection. Finally, they shared how they learned about local cultural activities and suggested ways to promote *After Hours* that may have flown under the radar of senior staff, such as advertising in alternative media. These sessions may not have cast as wide a net as formal focus groups, but they still delivered insights that greatly informed Gardner's strategy for *After Hours*, which attracted hundreds of new visitors from the very first evening. The total financial layout for Gardner's research? A few bills for pizza and beverages. (Gardner later conducted more formal audience research to fine-tune *After Hours*, as discussed in "Getting Visitor Feedback" on pp. 68–69.)

• • • • • • • •

Seattle Opera took a slightly more systematic but still low-cost approach to identify how to use social media and other technology to create a richer experience around the four-opera *Ring* cycle for its current audience. In mid-2009, the company emailed an online-survey invitation to 2,300 patron households that had purchased *Ring* tickets in the past.[8] The survey asked patrons about their online activities and the types of *Ring*-related digital content they would like to see. Given that Seattle Opera's *Ring* audience skews older—more than one-third are over age 65—staff expected to find low usage of digital content and social media, and questioned whether online initiatives should even be part of their engagement strategy for this audience. They were surprised when survey participants reported heavy usage of YouTube, podcasts, blogs, and Facebook. The survey also revealed that audiences were hungry for behind-the-scenes peeks at how operas are prepared for the stage. Knitting together these two insights, staff developed a series of online videos that showed different elements of the opera's preparation for the stage, as well as a simulated live feed of backstage activities that was broadcast in the lobby during intermissions. The survey results helped win broad support for the initiative from staff, even among those who had originally questioned it. That turned out to be a good move: audience surveys conducted after the *Ring* indicated that one-third of *Ring* patrons watched

---

8. Seattle Opera recognized that the sample was one of convenience. Surveys that are sent to people selected from a membership or box-office database do not capture a representative sample of the audience because they exclude audience members who did not buy their own ticket or who are not members. Such a selection bias might be acceptable if you are only interested in surveying ticket buyers, subscribers, or members, but it's a serious limitation when you are trying to understand the experience of all attendees.

· · · · · · · ·

the behind-the-scenes videos, and nearly 80 percent said that the videos enriched their operagoing experience.

There are a few caveats about doing research in-house. In trying to understand new audiences, staff may bring assumptions about their behavior that are based on the organization's work with current patrons, but that might not apply to newcomers. It can be hard to get the necessary fresh perspective. It's also best to steer clear of topics that are sensitive or politically charged. Staff with a vested interest might find it hard to set aside their biases, despite their best intentions. Moreover, research projects may face credibility challenges when they are carried out internally (i.e., by staffers who are not trained, impartial research professionals). Finally, although the financial outlay may be low, there is a lot of legwork involved. Staff at the Gardner not only spent considerable time recruiting participants for and organizing the discussion groups, but also prepared a formal discussion guide and wrote up the results—a necessary step to both clarify and communicate the research implications. At Seattle Opera, marketing staff wrote the survey themselves and reviewed hundreds of write-in comments to get an accurate read on just how many patrons cared about particular technologies or content. They also created a presentation with data so that they could effectively communicate the results to a skeptical in-house audience.

···5···

So Where Is This Going?
Thinking Through the
Relationship

*M*any of the case study organizations wanted new participants to not only walk through the door, but also experience their institution in specific ways. Much has been
written about moving audience interactions from transactions to relationships.[9] Organizations laid the groundwork for those relationships by
thinking through how audiences would interact with their organizations
and developing programs to fulfill their visions. By doing so, they created
the kinds of resonant experiences that build emotional bonds between
people and organizations.[10] They recognized that for that relationship to

---

9. For example, Suzanne M. Sato, "The Audience as Art," *American Theatre* (January
2005), 50–58; Ben Cameron, "Theatre Communications Group Field Letter, June 15,
2006," http://www.tcg.org/publications/fieldletter/july06_fieldletter.cfm; and Nina
Simon, *The Participatory Museum* (Santa Cruz, CA: Museum 2.0, 2010).

10. B. Joseph Pine II and James H. Gilmore, *The Experience Economy: Work Is Theatre
and Every Business a Stage* (Boston: Harvard Business School Press, 1999).

· · · · · · · ·

thrive, the needs of both parties have to be satisfied. On the one hand, the new audience has to find the relationship satisfying. On the other, the relationship needs to be grounded in the core values of the organization. That grounding helps the organization embrace the relationship and programs that are developed to support it.

Organizations laid the groundwork for relationships by thinking through how audiences would interact with them.

Steppenwolf Theatre Company wanted its single-ticket buyers to come to the theater more often, and did extensive research to understand what motivated them to attend performances. It discovered that single-ticket buyers and subscribers alike saw themselves as "lifelong learners" who enjoy pondering new ideas about the human condition. They came to Steppenwolf to be pushed out of their comfort zone. Staff envisioned a relationship with the audience that both satisfied its appetite to be challenged and adhered to the company's core values. Those values include the ensemble approach to creating theater through ongoing conversation and collaboration among the company's actors, directors, playwrights, and filmmakers. With that in mind, staff developed a concept of Steppenwolf as a "Public Square," a place where audience members and artists could interact and explore the meaning of the works on stage. Staff brought the concept to life through nightly post-show discussions, special thematic events, and a rich collection of online content, including podcasts, videos, and blog posts, in which ensemble members shared their observations and reflections about the company's productions. Single-ticket buyers responded favorably, with large numbers not only participating in the programs but also attending more performances than ever before.

· · · · · · · ·

Steppenwolf drew on an organizational strength—the ensemble's long-held practice of discussing works being prepared for the stage—to develop the Public Square and create a deeper relationship with its audience. It was a bit of a stretch, but completely in reach because it was grounded in the company's values and seemed like a natural evolution of the organization. Based on his experience running both large and small organizations, Columbia Business School professor William Pietersen believes institutions need to stretch in just this way when they envision a role for themselves in a changing world where, say, theater subscriptions are no longer enough to build loyalty:

> *The vision should be an extension of the firm's strategic choices, not a thing apart. A vision should involve stretch. The desired response should be, "Yes, that's where we want to go—but we can't get there by doing what we're doing today." Great visions motivate transformational behavior, not incrementalism.[11]*

The Isabella Stewart Gardner Museum was similarly inspired by its core values when developing a strategy to engage a new audience of young adults. The museum's educational philosophy is that critical thinking about art does not require knowledge of specific movements or artists. All that is necessary is thoughtful observation and discussion. Staff wanted to create an event for young, first-time visitors that engaged them with the museum's collection in such a way. At the same time, they recognized what its target audience wanted—a social event with friends after work.

---

11. William Pietersen, "Strategic Learning: A Leadership Process for Creating and Implementing Breakthrough Strategies." Working paper, Columbia Business School, 2005, p. 14.

· · · · · · · ·

The staff satisfied both needs with *Gardner After Hours*, an evening event built around the idea of a salon, a contemporary take on the art-focused soirees that the museum's founder hosted during her lifetime. They created a range of informal activities, such as brief gallery talks and games, that encouraged visitors to explore the museum's collection and share their observations as they explored artistic intent. The museum's atmospheric courtyard served as the backdrop for a bar and live music, but the social scene didn't upstage the art. More than 90 percent of *After Hours* attendees explored the galleries, with more than half saying it was their favorite activity of the night, according to exit surveys.

Neither Steppenwolf nor Gardner changed the art they presented in order to please their audiences.[12] They stayed true to who they were while at the same time adapting to a new audience with different needs. Indeed, Steppenwolf believes curatorial control is an essential part of its role in the Public Square. The company sets the direction of the conversation by determining which plays to produce and telling stories in a nuanced way, explains Artistic Director Martha Lavey.

Somewhat counterintuitively, Steppenwolf's new relationship with its audience has given its artists greater creative freedom. Knowing that

---

12. There are, however, examples of institutions that have expanded the work they present to be more inclusive of traditions or groups in their communities as part of a strategy to engage them, but still in a mission-fulfilling way. Diane Ragsdale, for example, describes Baltimore's Center Stage theater's commitment to producing work by African-American playwrights (to build a following among African Americans, who make up over 2/3 of Baltimore's population) and the Los Angeles Philharmonic's introduction of contemporary work to build a greater following among young people. See Diane Ragsdale, "Recreating Fine Arts Institutions," *Stanford Social Innovation Review* 7 (Fall 2009), 36–41.

········

Figure 6. Gardner After Hours
Photo by Derek Kouyoumjian; Courtesy of the Gardner Museum, Boston

its audience wants to be challenged, the ensemble has felt emboldened to make programming choices that it had hesitated about before. As Steppenwolf's Executive Director David Hawkanson explains:

> *We have more artistic confidence to do a wider and more challenging range of material. Our conversations about new seasons have changed from five years ago, when there was more of a consciousness about the presence of new vs. established plays. That's no longer on the table. Now our programming conversations revolve around the exploration of art and ideas, what projects the artists want to do, what our writers are trying to do.*

Even with the grant funding over, the programs at Steppenwolf and Gardner continue in full force and are still helping both organizations

· · · · · · · ·

build relationships with their audiences. Linda Garrison, former director of marketing and communications at Steppenwolf, believes that the Public Square succeeded because it was grounded so deeply in the theater's core values. "If [the vision] was not authentically a part of who the theater was, it would have never lasted," she says.

····6····

Providing Multiple
Ways In

*A*rts organizations overcame steep perceptual or practical barriers (or both) with new audiences by making it easier and more comfortable for them to participate. Some organizations let new audiences get acquainted with their art more informally, through low-key situations that fit their lifestyles or inclinations to participate. Other groups put their art in a context that was familiar to newcomers, in part to give them confidence that they would be able to appreciate it and to help them do so.

Making It Easier to Get to Know You

The Clay Studio offers ceramics classes for all skill levels, but its market research found that both financial and time constraints prevented a new target audience—urban professionals ages 25 to 45—from signing up. Most of its courses were 10-week classes that cost about $300. While that price may seem reasonable for the level of instruction offered—instructors typically have an MFA and decades of experience—focus group

· · · · · · · ·

participants who were unfamiliar with ceramic art said they were unlikely to invest so much money (and time) on something they weren't sure they would enjoy. Staff had heard similar pleas for shorter, low-cost classes from some current workshop participants.

Responding to audience demand, The Clay Studio gradually introduced different class formats to accommodate students with a range of schedules, financial resources, and interest levels. It complemented its 10-week course with a 5-week course, 3-hour weekend workshops, evening "social" workshops, drop-in family workshops, and more. In the process, it tripled enrollment in its classes and doubled tuition revenue over a five-year period that included the worst years of the recent economic recession. Interestingly, the organization also grew enrollment for its traditional 10-week course.

The Clay Studio saw such success because it developed multiple ways for its target audience to get to know it. Audience-building practitioner and expert Donna Walker-Kuhne calls this creating "points of entry… creating doors where none had existed before."[13] A person new to ceramics is unlikely to sign up for an expensive 10-week course right away, for instance, but may be open to sampling and exploring the organization in ways that do not entail a big commitment. She may even gradually become more involved and try the organization's traditional offerings, although that process is likely to be a slow one—most people don't become devotees overnight, or even over the course of a few years.

Fleisher Art Memorial also created more points of entry to reach its target audience, residents of its ethnically diverse neighborhood. Through

---

13. Donna Walker-Kuhne, *Invitation to the Party: Building Bridges to the Arts, Culture and Community* (New York: Theatre Communications Group, 2005), p. 12.

• • • • • • • •

market research, staff had learned that many new immigrants and other underserved groups in the community knew very little about Fleisher. As a result, they were unlikely to visit or consider sending their children to its on-site programs.

Fleisher is busting through these barriers by introducing itself to the community in many ways, on the theory that multiple experiences will build stronger connections. For instance, its mobile arts studio, ColorWheels, goes to local parks so children can make art and parents can get a feel for what Fleisher's on-site programs are like. It also hosts *ARTspiration!*, an annual arts festival in the neighborhood. These aren't

Figure 7. Fleisher Art Memorial's ColorWheels and ARTspiration! Festival

Photos courtesy of Fleisher Art Memorial, Philadelphia

· · · · · · · ·

"outreach programs" as they are sometimes thought of, in which bringing art to the community is the goal and the endpoint. Fleisher's aim is to gradually build a sense of familiarity with neighborhood residents that leads them to feel comfortable with the organization and eventually sign up for a class. Fleisher is also trying to make it easy for them to take that step when they're ready: For example, recognizing that many recent immigrants work in restaurants, it offers its popular bilingual introductory drawing class on Monday evening, when many of them have the night off.

Some may say that The Clay Studio and Fleisher created separate "watered down" versions of their regular programming to appeal to their target audiences. The staffs at both organizations were aware of the potential for such criticism and the risk that came with it. But they believed that introductory experiences were necessary to help people make that very difficult jump from bystander to participant. They hoped these initial interactions would lead to deeper forms of participation later on. While it would be great to find that one killer promotion that hooks an audience or turns newcomers into lifelong supporters, research suggests that is not how it works.[14] Sampling an art form, whether at a street fair, a drop-in workshop, or some other low-commitment, low-pressure situation, is a valuable way to kindle that process. No one would hold a match under a log and expect it to ignite right away. A small kindling fire is needed first.

---

14. For example, Anni Oskala, Emily Keaney, Tak Wing Chan, and Catherine Bunting, *Encourage Children Today to Build Audiences for Tomorrow* (London: Arts Council England, 2009); Nick Rabkin and E. C. Hedberg, *Arts Education in America: What the Declines Mean for Arts Participation* (Washington, D.C.: National Endowment for the Arts, 2011); Louise K. Stevens, *Motivating Opera Attendance: Comparative Qualitative Research in 10 North American Cities* (Washington, D.C.: Opera America, 2008).

. . . .

Making Your Art Feel Familiar

Research suggests that when people are unfamiliar with an organization or its art, they will be either indifferent about visiting because they aren't sure what to expect, or intimidated because they don't think they know enough to appreciate the experience and may even feel stupid. Either way, they're not coming. Several case study organizations neutralized the power of unfamiliarity by connecting to things that their target audiences already knew.

For instance, Minnesota Opera's promotion partner Ian Punnett recognized that the middle-aged women listening to his morning radio show probably weren't operagoers and therefore wouldn't get excited over a particular opera being by Donizetti or a certain singer starring in a lead role. In fact, such "insider" references might make them assume they would not know enough to appreciate the performance and cause them to tune out. Instead, Punnett used his radio announcements for Minnesota Opera to create what he called the "shortest line" between opera and his listeners. Punnett emphasized aspects of opera that newcomers could relate to instantly, talking up the intrigue or romantic elements of the plot, for example, or describing the elaborate sets. If he named a composer, he took care to provide a familiar context. In promotions for *The Pearl Fishers*, he told listeners that the composer Bizet had also done the better-known *Carmen*. Punnett's "shortest line" drew large numbers of his listeners to their first opera performance. (Minnesota Opera subsequently found that one or two positive experiences were not necessarily enough to turn most of these new audience members into frequent attendees. The greater challenge has been getting them to come to enough

· · · · · · · ·

performances so that they feel confident to make their own judgments about which operas they will enjoy without help from Punnett.)

Pacific Northwest Ballet realized the power of connecting to what audiences already know in trying to attract more teens and young adults. Originally, the company thought that contemporary dance would draw in this audience, but through focus group research (and confirmed by ticket receipts), it learned they actually gravitated to traditional story ballets. "They would say, '*Swan Lake* is safe; I've heard of it, I saw the movie,'" recalls Artistic Director Peter Boal.

Holly Arsenault has heard similar comments as executive director of Seattle's TeenTix, an organization that offers teens discount tickets to more than 50 local arts organizations:

> *We talk about teens' "intimidation factors" surrounding arts attendance a lot. One of the big ones is that they won't "get" it, won't know what to say about it to their friends afterward. In the case of dance, at least if it's a story ballet, then there's a narrative to follow. And, if it's a narrative that they are already with—like, say,* Romeo & Juliet—*so much the better.*

Teens and young adults in PNB's focus groups also said they stayed away because they didn't know much about the company or its artists, or even what to expect at a performance. Based on that insight, staff created a series of online videos that, in the words of Executive Director Ellen Walker, offered "multiple ways in to see what we do every day." The videos introduced audiences to PNB's (mostly young) dancers and gave an idea of what they would see onstage. The company further tried to make itself familiar to young audiences by inviting teenage reviewers from TeenTix to its performances. The online reviews of these TeenTix writers helped thousands of their peers learn what PNB's productions

• • • • • • • •

had to offer people like them. Thanks to these and other related efforts, PNB's ticket sales to teens via TeenTix doubled to more than 2,000 tickets per season within four years.

There's an interesting catch, however, in employing video to build familiarity with new audiences. Common sense suggests that online media is most likely accessed by people already close to your organization and art form. People who get your email blasts, follow your Twitter feed, or like you on Facebook probably already have some experience with your organization. Even if a potential audience member stumbles upon your videos on YouTube, why would she watch them? Indeed, that is exactly what PNB's neighbor, Seattle Opera, found. It experimented with a variety of digital media, including behind-the-scenes videos that were a hit with its current audience but had considerably fewer uptakes among newcomers, who often did not know the videos existed. That said, both Seattle Opera and PNB increased their odds of newcomers finding and clicking on a video because they committed to producing a regular stream of new content. Producing the videos in-house has made a high level of output feasible and sustainable at both organizations.

....7....

Aligning the Organization
Around the Strategy

"For a strategy to be supported and acted upon, it needs to live in the hearts and minds of employees," writes Columbia Business School professor and business leader Willie Pietersen.[15] Organizational alignment around a strategy clarifies direction, builds buy-in, instills a sense of urgency, and expedites decision making. Unfortunately, arts organizations often do not give enough time or attention to it because it seems tangential to the "real" work of designing and deploying audience-engagement programs.

Alignment clarifies strategic direction, builds buy-in, instills a sense of urgency, and expedites decision making.

Among the 54 organizations that received WEA funding, some treated their audience-building initiatives as side projects, peripheral to their core activities. The initiatives got little attention outside of a marketing or education department, and the lack of cross-departmental coordination prevented them from picking up steam. In some cases, not all staff

---

15. Willie Pietersen, *Strategic Learning* (Hoboken, NJ: John Wiley & Sons, 2010), p. 159.

recognized the target audience as important to the organization, and their indifference or resistance made it impossible to build momentum. The initiatives, as a result, ceased when foundation funding ran out.

Initiatives at other organizations, meanwhile, flourished because the entire staff shared a commitment to attracting a certain audience and an understanding of how they would go about it. They knew the kind of relationship that the organization wanted to have with the audience, believed it was critical to the institution's future, and understood their individual roles in making it succeed. This alignment didn't just happen. It resulted because senior leaders supported the initiative and made a deliberate effort to rally the organization behind it.

Steppenwolf Theatre Company Executive Director David Hawkanson believed so strongly in gaining internal buy-in for the Public Square concept (described in "Thinking Through the Relationship," pp. 43–45) that he took managers from several key departments on a multiday retreat to discuss its purpose and goals. He recognized that an abstract concept like the Public Square would only come to life if staff embraced its potential to transform the company's relationship with single-ticket buyers and could envision how it would play out. Once they understood that, they could start to think about how their day-to-day work in marketing, development, production, operations, and other departments could impact its success.

Steppenwolf's efforts did not stop there. For Hawkanson, the retreat was not about delivering marching orders to troops, but starting a conversation among staff about the Public Square and their individual roles in building it. The resulting back-and-forth dialogue sent a clear signal that the Public Square was important to the organization and helped

· · · · · · · ·

staff develop not just a sense of clarity about it, but a sense of ownership too. At organization-wide meetings held five times a year, each department discussed its audience-engagement activities in terms of the Public Square.

"We managed to get everyone in the same place on the Public Square and ensured that Steppenwolf speaks on these issues with a very consistent voice," says Hawkanson. The alignment at Steppenwolf was so pervasive that every staff member interviewed for the case study, regardless of seniority or tenure, spontaneously described his or her work in relation to two ideas: the importance of drawing audiences out of their comfort zones and Steppenwolf's role in the Public Square to create theater, invite the audience to discuss it, and gradually improve the audience's ability to critically assess the plays. The result is an integrated effort around the ideals of the Public Square. For instance:

- The front-of-house staff understood that their job was to make attendees feel welcome as members of the Steppenwolf community.

- The promotions team, recognizing that audience members saw themselves as lifelong learners, created ads that highlighted thematic elements of the company's productions, rather than logistical details.

- The marketing team facilitated audience participation by producing online videos, blogs, and podcasts that featured artistic staff members sharing their personal explorations of the work on stage.

- The artists volunteered their time to make the digital content, and saw the audience as "with them" in the process of creating theater.

· · · · · · · ·

The broad support ensured that organizational activities built on one another. Artistic and marketing department staff found themselves working together toward a common purpose. In fact, both the marketing director at the time, Linda Garrison, and Artistic Director Martha Lavey saw the fulfillment of the Public Square as central to their roles.

Broad support ensured that organizational activities built on one another.

In his classic management book, *Leading Change*,[16] Harvard Business School professor John P. Kotter asserts that analogies or metaphors like the Public Square can help leaders effectively convey an organization's strategy to employees. Fleisher Art Memorial didn't use a metaphor, but rather a compelling and memorable mantra that encapsulated its activities to engage recent immigrants and other underserved residents in its ethnically diverse neighborhood. "Come to Us, Show Us, Welcome Us" described what focus groups of neighborhood residents said Fleisher could do to encourage them to take classes at its facility: take the first step by meeting them in familiar local settings, vividly explain and demonstrate the activities available at the organization, and, should they visit, make them feel welcome when they walked through the door. Magda Martinez, director of programs at Fleisher, says the mantra has become a "directional compass" guiding the organization's efforts with this audience.

The initiative's catchphrase also guided internal conversations about the initiative. Joseph Gonzales, Fleisher's manager of research and com-

---

16. John P. Kotter, *Leading Change* (Boston: Harvard Business School Press, 1996).

• • • • • • • •

munity engagement strategies at the time, led brown-bag information sessions with staff across the organization to explain the initiative and the implications for their work. Some staff members at these meetings openly questioned Fleisher's continued dedication to its current audience and the relevance of their own roles. These conversations were not easy, and at times they became emotional, but leaders believed that all staff concerns should be addressed respectfully and transparently to prevent issues from festering and undermining success. They emphasized that this wasn't a zero-sum game where one audience won and the other lost. Current visitors would continue to play a vital role as Fleisher expanded its audience to be more inclusive.

Fleisher's leaders recognized that they couldn't expect staff to know how to serve an audience with whom they had little experience. They hired an outside facilitator to train staff in understanding multicultural perspectives (including how their own cultures influenced their worldviews) and interacting with people of diverse backgrounds. The entire staff and even some board members also visited neighborhood gathering places, community organizations, and religious institutions to understand better how to serve their constituents, and participated in workshops to refine their strategy for collaborating with community groups.

Organizational alignment may not produce anything tangible right away, but the intangible results—focus, a shared sense of purpose and motivation to achieve that purpose—give initiatives momentum. To achieve it, Steppenwolf and Fleisher made sure they could answer "yes" to both of these questions:

· · · · · · · ·

- Do all leaders and staff members understand their roles and responsibilities in support of the audience development goal (or initiative)?

- Does everyone understand why the initiative is important and grasp its full implications for the organization?

Their efforts ensured that their initiatives lasted long after the grant funding did. Fleisher's "Come to Us, Show Us, Welcome Us" and Steppenwolf's Public Square have remained part of the daily discourse at both organizations since their funding ended, and continue to play important roles in helping them build their audiences.

· · · · · · · ·

Strong Visions Can Invite Resistance

Pursuing a new audience is likely to make staff members—particularly those whose roles involve serving current audiences—nervous about the security of their jobs and responsibilities. Addressing the topic of organizational change, business writer Richard Luecke warns that some staff members "may perceive change as endangering their livelihoods, their perks, their workplace social arrangements or their status in the organization. Others know that their specialized skills will be rendered less valuable."[1]

Visions that present a clear direction and force organizations to make choices are most likely to provoke such nervousness and staff resistance. Business leader and consultant Hugh Davidson has analyzed reactions to these strong visions at more than 100 for-profit and non-profit organizations. "Strong visions...excite strong emotions," he notes. "They are challenging, uncomfortable, nail biting and polarizing. Some people will be so opposed that they will wish to leave. Consensus may be impossible to achieve, but the critical mass of people who believe strongly in the vision will then turn it into reality."[2]

1. Richard Luecke, *Managing Change and Transition* (Boston: Harvard Business School Press, 2003), p. 74.

2. Hugh Davidson, *The Committed Enterprise*, 2nd Edition (Oxford: Elsevier, 2004), p. 104.

···*8*···

Building in Learning

By its nature, audience building typically involves trying to attract newcomers whose barriers, interests, and preferences are not well understood. While the case study organizations did extensive up-front research to develop programs that would appeal to their target audiences, not even the best research can predict response with complete accuracy. For that reason, many of them followed a continuous cycle of learning as their initiatives unfolded—they experimented, assessed, and fine-tuned their programs to achieve maximum effectiveness. The most flexible organizations came to think of their action plans as starting points in a long journey. They evaluated and readjusted tactics as necessary, knowing that the long-term audience-building goal was more important than executing exactly to plan.

Learning from Experience on the Ground

The organizations that were studied had the advantage of funds that let them take risks they might not otherwise have taken, but they still recognized the finite resources at their disposal and tried to make the most of them. Some of them did pilot tests or "soft launches" of programs to

· · · · · · · ·

lower the risk of expending significant resources until they had some evidence that their ideas would gain traction.

The Contemporary Jewish Museum (CJM), for example, used its limited resources to experiment with a range of new programs for families. The museum's move into a new building more than 20 times the size of its former facility dialed up the pressure to ensure a steady flow of visitors, but The CJM wasn't sure which of its ideas would click with families. Instead of placing large bets on untested programs, staff rolled out several initiatives with a prototype approach, then evaluated and recalibrated them as necessary to achieve the desired results, and went big with the improved program.[17]

Not all made the cut. For example, one early idea to build a base of returning visitors was a "Family Passport" that rewarded families who made multiple visits. The CJM planned to distribute the passports to students at local schools. They pictured a somewhat elaborate design for the actual passport, with a holder and a guide to museum activities. Before spending money on the design and production, staff piloted a simpler free family pass program, and hit a snag: Only 1 percent of the passes were redeemed. Staff modified the pass, thinking that the design was a

---

17. Connie Wolf, who was The CJM's CEO at the time, likens this approach to Jim Collins's "fire bullets, then cannonballs" principle (see Jim Collins and Morten T. Hansen, *Great by Choice: Uncertainty, Chaos, and Luck—Why Some Thrive Despite Them All* [New York: Harper Business, 2011]). The principle uses the metaphor of firing a cannon with a limited amount of gunpowder. Using all the gunpowder and missing would mean missing for good. A wiser approach would be to first fire bullets using small amounts of gunpowder, recalibrate until the target is hit and then use the remaining gunpowder to fire the cannonball.

. . . .

potential problem, and also added an expiration date to motivate use, but redemption was still low. At the same time, they were seeing an unexpectedly huge success from a more personal form of outreach, partnerships with preschool directors to bring communities of parents and their preschoolers together at The CJM on specific days. Keeping its eye on the ultimate goal of engaging families, The CJM shifted funds away from the family pass program to build similar (successful) partnerships with elementary schools and the San Francisco Public Library based on shared objectives. For an iterative approach like this to work, organizations need good data and insight into which programs are working and which ones need adjustment. They also need to be open to testing, modifying, and shifting efforts rapidly.

Other organizations relied on the eyes and ears of front-line staff to detect areas in need of improvement. In the early days of *Gardner After Hours*, staff at the Isabella Stewart Gardner Museum huddled for regular feedback sessions after each month's event to discuss it while it was still fresh in their minds. The group included on-the-ground personnel such as the concessions manager, security guards, concert manager, visitor services, and membership staff members. Each gave their take of the event in order to diagnose problems, propose solutions, build buy-in for those solutions, and make sure that one or more staff members took ownership of their implementation at the next *After Hours*. Subsequent feedback sessions reviewed the impact of those fixes. While many of the improvements were logistical, such as reducing wait times for food or beverages, others involved changes in programming to enhance audience participation. For instance, when staff members discovered how crowded their

. . . .

twice-nightly introductory gallery talks were, they added four more. That modification successfully reduced the size of each group, thus making the talks more interactive for attendees.

Getting Visitor Feedback

Gardner complemented its staff evaluations by regularly surveying visitors during the first few years of *After Hours*. These surveys measured who was attending and how they experienced the event and its programs.

The research was critical for three reasons. First, staff wanted to ensure they were attracting their target demographic of young adults. Second, they were wary of the tendency for art to get lost at events like *After Hours* and wanted to know if the evening's social aspects were upstaging the collection. Finally, staff tried many untested ideas for programming at the event, all of which took time and resources to develop. They needed to understand which activities drew the most participants and which ones were liked best. The survey was a low-cost (albeit labor-intensive) way to meet these three objectives.

The surveys confirmed that the event was reaching its target demographic. In the first year, two-thirds of visitors were 18 to 34 years old, with nearly three-quarters falling into that age group the subsequent year. The survey also found that the Gardner's art collection was the evening's main attraction. In fact, attendees said that exploring the galleries was their most popular and most satisfying activity. Many reported participating in and enjoying short, informal activities such as interactive talks around a few works of art, so the staff expanded those offerings. When other activities such as a self-guided tour got less traction even after re-

. . . .

peated attempts to improve it, they were dropped so that staff could focus their limited time on developing programs that had proven popular.

Twice during the event's first year, the Gardner also engaged outside consultants to interview groups of attendees. The interviewers asked visitors why they had attended *After Hours*, what they did at the event, how the *After Hours* environment affected their experience, and what changes could make the event more appealing. Among other things, the researchers found that the art stimulated conversation among groups of visitors, and the presence of young volunteers and museum activities drew people into the collection. That finding prompted staff to expand its corps of young volunteers. Some guests also expressed disappointment that there were not enough opportunities to meet new people. Staff responded by creating more social opportunities, such as a series of "gallery games" where visitors interact with their friends and others as they examine the art collection. The games turned out to be a hit. Taken together, the staff meetings, visitor surveys, and visitor interviews provided clear visibility into how *After Hours* was running and informed progressive improvements that led to a more satisfying experience for a growing audience.[18]

Seattle Opera used formal research to assess whether its use of online technology was engaging different audience segments. Most arts organizations had little experience reaching audiences through digital media in 2008, so there were no established best practices for the company to

---

18. For example, the number of visitors who said that their experience at *After Hours* made them much more interested in visiting during regular hours went from 51 percent in the first year to 77 percent in the second year, and the number who said they would be extremely likely to recommend *After Hours* went from 71 percent to 75 percent. Attendance at the event went from approximately 500 visitors each night during its first year to 700 in the third year, and it regularly surpasses that figure today.

....

follow when it launched an effort to explore how digital and social media could enhance the operagoing experience. Accordingly, staff made organizational learning a key objective of their technological experiments. Each year of its four-year grant period, the company launched a different suite of online engagement tools, such as videos, podcasts, Kindle applications, and event live streaming, and surveyed its audience three times to gauge their reactions. Through that feedback, staff developed companywide expertise about which digital content and technology tools worked with different audience groups.

For example, the research demonstrated the tremendous appeal and impact of behind-the-scenes videos that the staff created in the first year for a production of the *Ring* cycle. One-third of *Ring* attendees watched the online videos, and of those, 80 percent said it enhanced their experience of going to the performance. Staff hadn't intended to produce behind-the-scenes videos for every production going forward, but based on the feedback, they changed their plans. The videos continue to attract large numbers of enthusiastic viewers today.

The surveys also revealed important information that would have been impossible to obtain from web analytics alone. The research showed, for instance, that different audience segments accessed different content. Audience members attending the *Ring* viewed behind-the-scenes videos but were much less likely to watch introductory ones about opera, which was the content *most* accessed by other patrons.

Seattle Opera discovered what wasn't working, too. For example, the research revealed that fewer than 10 percent of audience members used interactive tools, such as an application that let them review and share scenes from operas online. That insight enabled staff to make quick, in-

· · · · · · · ·

telligent decisions to focus their resources less on tools designed to build interactive communities and more on tools that helped audience members learn about what goes into making opera.

Audience research can also help arts organizations diagnose specific trouble spots and figure out how to overcome them. Minnesota Opera successfully attracted hundreds of first-time operagoers by partnering with a radio personality who shared his enthusiasm for opera and offered free tickets to performances he would be attending. Anecdotal evidence suggested that these newcomers enjoyed themselves, but Minnesota Opera had trouble moving them along a series of graduated promotional offers that was supposed to lead eventually to a full-price ticket purchase. It identified the issue immediately because it was fortunate enough to have a database administrator who built and managed a system for engaging and tracking comp-ticket recipients.

Minnesota Opera conducted focus groups with comp-ticket recipients to diagnose what was impeding subsequent ticket purchase. It discovered an important purchase barrier that surprisingly had little connection to ticket prices or satisfaction with the performance. Turns out, newcomers weren't familiar enough with the art form to know which opera they might like, and they were not about to take a financial risk to see something they knew nothing about, even if they enjoyed their initial experience and wanted to return. The free tickets had been for a specific performance of a specific opera on a specific date, eliminating the need to choose. And the research suggested that the recommendation from a trusted source (the radio personality) had made them feel more confident that they might enjoy the performance. The findings informed some new promotions that Minnesota Opera has tried to help first-time buyers

· · · · · · · ·

overcome their indecision. For example, a post-performance "impulse buy" subscription regularly sells 100 new subscriptions at *each performance* where it is offered.

Evaluating Broader Objectives

The organizations studied mostly focused on attendance data—ticket purchases, visits, or enrollment in classes and workshops—to gauge the effectiveness of their initiatives. That is understandable since visits, especially repeat visits, are an important measure of audience participation. In addition, many funders typically ask grantees to provide this type of data. But a few case study organizations went beyond attendance statistics and explored the perceptions and subjective experiences of their target audiences.

Just as RAND's *New Framework* can help determine which barriers to target with specific audiences (see "Determining What Kinds of Barriers Need to Be Removed," pp. 19–27), it can also guide evaluation efforts. So, for example, organizations looking to diversify might track changes in how an audience perceives them. Fleisher Art Memorial had attendance data in hand proving that its efforts to attract more residents of its surrounding neighborhood were beginning to have some impact. Enrollment of local children in its on-site programs rose 50 percent during the four years of its initiative. That was very good news, but three years of visitor surveys suggested that the ethnic composition of the audience was not budging. Staff knew that attracting a broad cross-section of residents could take several years, and that they would first need to change perceptions that their organization was elitist. Accordingly, their visitor surveys also tracked perceptions of the organization's interest in

· · · · · · · ·

serving diverse groups. The results were encouraging—72 percent of visitors in 2012 said Fleisher cared about serving residents of the surrounding neighborhood, up from 56 percent in 2009. Half of visitors surveyed in 2012 also said that the institution cared about people whose cultural heritage is from outside the U.S., up from 36 percent in 2009. Staff take that as a sign that they are moving in the right direction.

Many organizations wanted to develop stronger relationships with their audiences, so they explored what audience members thought about their particular institution and its role in their lives. Perhaps the organization that did so most directly was The Clay Studio. As previously discussed, the organization tripled its enrollment in classes and workshops in five years, and attracted a new audience of young adults. Intent on understanding and strengthening the appeal of The Clay Studio for this new audience, staff commissioned in-depth interviews with first-time visitors under age 45. The interviews explored their motivations for coming, their experiences while visiting, and their perceptions and the emotional benefits of taking part in different programs. Staff were pleased to hear The Clay Studio most often described as "fun," "creative," and "inspiring." Interviewees voluntarily described The Clay Studio in terms of activities they could do there, not what the organization was or what it offered. This experiential focus dovetailed with what staff had heard in earlier focus groups (discussed on pp. 36–38 in "Identifying What Excites Newcomers") and gave them the green light to position the organization with young adults as a social and friendly place where people have unique experiences exploring the process of making ceramic art. In this way, the organization is looking to carve out for itself a unique place in the lives of this new audience.

....9....

Preparing for Success

*I*n a best-case scenario, an audience-building initiative attracts large numbers of new visitors. It is hard to anticipate, however, some of the growing pains and challenges that come with that success.

For starters, it can strain organizational capacity. The Clay Studio had to respond quickly when the new formats for its classes and workshops attracted hundreds of newcomers. The organization needed to not only ensure that first-time visitors had a good experience, but also build capacity to serve them and figure out the messages that would work best in subsequent marketing to them. On top of that, staff implemented a new database to track its growing visitor base—a great asset to have, but one that took considerable time to learn how to use. "It takes time to figure out how to process all that work," explains Vice President Jennifer Martin. "You're going to make mistakes." Vigilance and flexibility have helped The Clay Studio cope well with the success of its audience-building initiative. But staff admit that they often feel stretched trying to find enough hours in the day to handle the increased responsibilities.

The staff at Minnesota Opera felt similarly stretched as they tried to grow their audience of women ages 35 to 60 who were new to opera. Focus groups had indicated that these women enjoyed attending a performance on a free ticket and were willing to pay to go again, but their lack of familiarity with opera made it hard for them to decide which one to go see. The company's marketing materials worked well with veteran operagoers who had the experience to pick an opera based on its name or composer, but not with novices. Knowing that an opera was called *Roberto Devereux* or that the composer was Donizetti did not have much significance for them. As a result, staff spent significant time and resources to create a unique marketing strategy for new operagoers, in addition to producing its regular marketing materials for its existing audience.

The case study organizations also found that it can take time to perfect internal coordination to ensure that a new audience's needs are met. Soon after launching its initiative to encourage greater participation from residents in its ethnically diverse neighborhood, Fleisher Art Memorial came up with the idea of inviting musicians and artists of Mexican heritage to participate at *ARTspiration!*, its annual community arts festival. Fleisher's marketing team advertised the event in Spanish-language newspapers that were locally distributed in areas with large Mexican populations. The idea paid off, with many Spanish-speaking families coming to the festival. Problem was, staff had not fully considered what these visitors would need to get the most out of the experience. There were no signs in Spanish, and no one at the festival's information booth spoke the language. Some attendees left disappointed. The organization rectified the situation in future years, and thanks to such improvements and a continued push to attract members of its diverse community, it has seen festival attendance from its surrounding neighborhood quadruple to more than 1,000 people.

· · · · · · · ·

Newcomers Welcome?

Fleisher's lack of support for Spanish speakers at its arts festival was simply an oversight—staff members had little experience serving them and were learning as they went. Sometimes, however, staff may question the increased presence of newcomers. It could be out of concern for the organization's artistic direction, its ability to serve multiple audiences, or a general discomfort with the unknown. Most of the case study organizations, including those that spent considerable time aligning their staffs behind the initiative, reported some degree of friction as they adapted to serve a new audience. While it was never easy to resolve, staff found that addressing concerns directly in an environment of respect—and recognizing them as reflections of strong affection for beloved institutions— moved the organization forward.

Magda Martinez, Fleisher's director of programs, recalls one staff member who voiced concerns in a meeting about the organization's plans to let teens who were not participating in its regular programs drop in after school to make art:

> She kept saying, "These kids, those kids." I couldn't thank her enough because there was tension all around that table, but she was honest enough to say, "Look, they're going to come in and mess up my building." I said, "You're right. There is a chance that could happen. So, what are we going to do so it doesn't? What do you need me to tell the Teen Lounge staff and the kids up front so that they understand what our expectations are for the building?" It was great to have that conversation because it allowed us to be proactive as opposed to people saying later, "See? I told you that was going to happen."

Pacific Northwest Ballet took the initiative to defuse tensions before

· · · · · · · ·

they arose with current audience members as large numbers of teens began attending its performances. The company sold discounted tickets to teens for seats spread throughout the hall, leading some to find themselves next to older adults who questioned how they got seats usually held by longtime subscribers. PNB responded with an announcement in its programs (Figure 8) that explained the teen ticket program and showed how much it valued this new audience.

There is also the risk that new marketing can alienate current audiences. The Clay Studio is still trying to navigate the balancing act of speaking to different audiences looking for different things from the organization. While staff have used tongue-in-cheek phrases such as "I ♥ Dirt" and "Get Dirty" in advertising targeted to a younger, hipper crowd, they are careful never to poke fun at the institution's activities, knowing that doing so could jeopardize their relationship with collectors of ceramic art and longtime students who appreciate the Studio's serious side. "We don't want the integrity of the organization or mission to go," says Vice President Jennifer Martin.

Surprisingly, the challenges that come with success are some of the most difficult to resolve. Grappling with change and the unknown can easily tax both capabilities and emotions. The continuous adjustment and adaptation required for audience-building initiatives suggest that they do not really have an "end point." Instead, they constantly evolve as audiences and relationships change, and as organizations continue to learn. Even the most successful initiatives need "care and feeding," says Julie Crites, formerly director of program planning at the Isabella Stewart Gardner Museum, adding, "You can't rest on your laurels."

· · · · · · · ·

Welcome Teens!

Wondering who that young ballet-goer is, sitting in that seat next to you? They could very well be a member of Seattle Center's Teen Tix program. Since the inception of this city-run arts access program for teenagers, Pacific Northwest Ballet has been a proud and passionate participant. Now in its sixth year of operation, Teen Tix provides Seattle-area teenagers with access to 37 arts organizations in an effort to engage young people in Seattle's vibrant cultural scene. Teen Tix membership enables teenagers to purchase day-of-show tickets to music, dance, theater, and arts events for only $5.

For more information, visit Seattle Center's Teen Tix webpage at www.seattlecenter.com/teentix... or just lean over and ask the teen sitting next to you.

Figure 8. PNB Program Announcement Welcoming Teens

Courtesy of Pacific Northwest Ballet, Seattle

In Conclusion

·······

Building Momentum

Most arts managers agree that few people become dedicated audience members after a single visit, no matter how much they enjoy it. All evidence about sustained arts engagement suggests that it springs from a comfort level and special relationship developed over multiple experiences. Audience-building programs take on the herculean task of trying to recreate and compress a process that naturally takes years. Newcomers need to have many rewarding experiences, most likely with several sides of an institution. Accordingly, it is not surprising that two overarching themes connect the nine effective practices described above:

Successful initiatives created meaningful connections.

The case study organizations targeted audiences that fit them (practice 2), that leaders and staff believed could bring vitality to the organization, and that the organization could satisfy. By focusing on a specific audience, the organizations were able to tailor their strategies to that group's interests and lifestyles. These strategies first broke down the barriers that kept the audience away (practice 3), then built a meaningful connection with them to encourage repeat visits. Some organizations went as far as to articulate a vision of the relationship they wanted to have with

· · · · · · · ·

the audience, allowing them to express their missions in new contexts (practice 5). They created many opportunities for their audience to get to know them (practice 6), including low-key gateway experiences that let audience members sample activities in ways that were comfortable. In figuring out how to make those connections, the organizations listened to their audiences and used that information to design relevant programs and resonant marketing campaigns (practice 4).

Successful initiatives received sustained attention from both leadership and staff.

That sustained attention was necessary given the long time span and broad organizational involvement that audience-building initiatives require. First, it often takes time for organizations to learn what really clicks with a certain audience. Then it takes additional time to gain traction with that audience and develop a strong following, even with a well-designed and executed strategy.

Organizations had a better chance at sustaining attention when their audience-building initiatives were rooted in a sense of urgency that came by acknowledging a weighty challenge or opportunity for their future (practice 1). The most successful ones aligned staff behind their audience-building strategies and tactics (practice 7). Leaders and staff all understood the importance of the initiative and their individual roles in implementing it. The organizations also strived for continuous improvement, using on-the-ground experience and audience research to learn which aspects of their initiative were working and what could be better (practice 8). Finally, they monitored their institution's ability to handle

· · · · · · · ·

new visitors and made adjustments as necessary (practice 9).

Our hope is that the successes of the organizations profiled here can help other institutions make strategic choices for their audience-building programs and execute more effectively. That said, highlighting only the effective practices risks oversimplifying, and can give the impression that everything worked all the time. The truth is that the journeys of many of the case study organizations were quite messy, and not all were complete successes. But when things did not go as planned, they accepted such setbacks as part of the process. It wasn't always easy, especially when successes came slowly. What seemed to keep them going was an understanding that building repeat attendance can take years—a recognition that it takes time to learn how to work with a new audience and, in turn, for a new audience to see an institution as a place where it belongs.

Appendix

· · · · · · · ·

The Wallace Excellence Award Case Studies

T he Wallace Excellence Awards financially supported audience-building programs at 54 organizations in six cities that represented different forms of performing and visual arts. The groups targeted different audiences and used different audience-building strategies. Ten of the organizations were chosen for case studies, selected in part because of their success in two areas:

1. Measurable growth in attendance, such as an increase in visitors to a museum, students taking art classes, or audience members at performances

2. The audience-building programs continued to be successful after the funding concluded because the organizations remained committed to them and had developed the capabilities to support them.

This is a definition of convenience, chosen in part because all of the initiatives could be evaluated against these criteria. We do not wish to imply that arts organizations should *only* strive for these two measures of success.

Moreover, success was not the only criterion for inclusion. Some of the case study organizations achieved mixed results, but their experiences still provided informative material for analysis. There were also other WEA grantees not selected for the case studies that attained strong results from highly effective programs.

· · · · · · · ·

Case Study Organization Profiles

Boston Lyric Opera

- Location: Boston
- Founded in 1976, merged with Opera New England in 1998 to become the largest opera company in New England
- Produces four operas each season
- Audience: 22,300 annually
- Annual operating budget: $7 million

The Clay Studio

- Location: Philadelphia
- Founded in 1974 by five ceramic artists in need of a workspace for themselves and other recent art school graduates
- Offers ceramic art classes and workshops, artists' programs, exhibitions, and special events
- Audience: 30,000 visitors annually, 3,600 students in its workshops and classes, over 1,800 in Claymobile outreach, and more than 10,000 in new community outreach events
- Annual operating budget: $1.7 million

The Contemporary Jewish Museum

- Location: San Francisco
- Founded in 1984
- A non-collecting institution that partners with national and international institutions to present timely and relevant exhibitions

· · · · · · · ·

- Audience: 125,000 visitors annually (slightly less than half are Jewish)
- Annual operating budget: $6.5 million

Fleisher Art Memorial

- Location: Philadelphia
- Founded in 1898 by industrialist Samuel S. Fleisher, who held art classes for lower-income neighborhood boys
- Offers classes, exhibitions, and community-based programming in the visual arts
- Audience: 17,000 annually
- Annual operating budget: $2.5 million

Isabella Stewart Gardner Museum

- Location: Boston
- Founded in 1903 by art patron and collector Isabella Stewart Gardner
- Houses Gardner's personal art collection of more than 2,500 paintings, sculptures, tapestries, furniture, manuscripts, rare books, and decorative arts
- Audience: 218,000 annually
- Annual operating budget: $14.7 million

Minnesota Opera

- Location: Minneapolis
- Founded: 1963, merged with St. Paul Opera in 1975
- Produces five operas each season, each with five to eight performances

· · · · · · · ·

- Audience: 49,000
- Annual operating budget: $10.1 million

Pacific Northwest Ballet
- Location: Seattle
- Founded in 1972
- Produces six mixed-repertory or full-length ballets each season, for a total of 100 performances
- Audience: More than 250,000 annually
- Annual operating budget: $23 million

San Francisco Girls Chorus
- Location: San Francisco
- Founded in 1978
- The Chorus consists of 45 girls ages 12 to 18 who present a four-concert season as well as a holiday concert, guest appearances, and international tours. The ensemble is supported by a Chorus School training program comprised of 350 singers ages 5 through 12.
- Audience: 4,865 annually
- Annual operating budget: $2.2 million

Seattle Opera
- Location: Seattle
- Founded in 1963
- Produces five operas with approximately 35 to 40 performances per season

· · · · · · · ·

- Audience: More than 100,000
- Annual operating budget: $23 million

Steppenwolf Theatre Company

- Location: Chicago
- Founded in 1976 by a collective of actors
- Current ensemble consists of 44 artists who produce more than 13 productions annually, for a total of more than 700 performances
- Audience: 200,000 annually
- Annual operating budget: $15.5 million

About the Author

Bob Harlow, PhD, is a social psychologist and statistician who develops research programs that help organizations more deeply understand their target audiences. He has partnered with marketing managers and senior executives at some of the world's largest companies and leading nonprofit organizations to develop brand, communications, and operations strategies. He has held senior and management positions at IBM and at market research consulting groups such as Yankelovich Partners, RONIN, and KRC, and currently leads Bob Harlow Research and Consulting, LLC, a market research consulting organization.

Bob has written hundreds of surveys and conducted hundreds of focus groups and interviews with broad audiences in 30 countries. He has more than a dozen scholarly publications in social psychology and research methods, and is the lead author of The Wallace Foundation publication series Wallace Studies in Building Arts Audiences. He has a PhD from Princeton University in social psychology and completed the postdoctoral program in quantitative analysis at New York University's Stern School of Business and Graduate School of Arts and Science.

Wallace Studies in Building Arts Audiences

· · · · · · · ·

CULTIVATING THE NEXT GENERATION OF ART LOVERS

How Boston Lyric Opera Sought to Create
Greater Opportunities
for Families to Attend Opera

MORE THAN JUST A PARTY

How the Isabella Stewart Gardner Museum Boosted
Participation by Young Adults

ATTRACTING AN ELUSIVE AUDIENCE

How the San Francisco Girls Chorus Is Breaking Down
Stereotypes and Generating Interest among
Classical Music Patrons

BUILDING DEEPER RELATIONSHIPS

How Steppenwolf Theatre Company Is Turning
Single-Ticket Buyers into Repeat Visitors

Forthcoming titles in 2014–2015
will include case studies of
audience-building programs by:

THE CLAY STUDIO
THE CONTEMPORARY JEWISH MUSEUM
FLEISHER ART MEMORIAL
MINNESOTA OPERA
PACIFIC NORTHWEST BALLET
SEATTLE OPERA